Georgie Bailey

DJ Bazzer's Year 6 Disco

(Or: The Vindication of the Tortured Artist)

Produced in association with ChewBoy Productions

Baz is the resident DJ of Brigdale Primary. Next week, it's the Year 6 Leavers' Disco: the biggest gig of the year. With a mighty setlist of early-noughties bangers cued up, Baz is raring to go for the event of a lifetime. That is, until their old school rival barges his way back onto the scene, forcing Baz to recollect the things he'd kept buried for years, and face up to moments in his past that will define his future…

Join Baz in the multimedia, solo adventure of the century: DJ BAZZER's YEAR 6 DISCO, exploring childhood dreams that never wake up, the things that keep you up at night and the toxicity of comparing ourselves to others. As Baz traverses through the nostalgic sounds of his childhood, he asks the audience to consider the hopes they had for growing up, and what it means to be alive through a journey of Magaluf rooftop raves, hospital wards and the glow stick laden school halls of years gone by.

Salamander Street

PLAYS

First published in 2021 by Salamander Street Ltd.
(info@salamanderstreet.com)

DJ Bazzer's Year 6 Disco and *Tethered* © Georgie Bailey, 2021

ISBN: 9781914228490

10 9 8 7 6 5 4 3 2 1

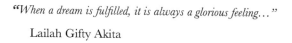

"When a dream is fulfilled, it is always a glorious feeling…"

Lailah Gifty Akita

"*…but who is that on the other side of you?*"

T.S. Eliot

Acknowledgements

DJ Bazzer's Year 6 Disco was originally performed at the Golden Goose Theatre, Camberwell in September 2021.

Originally directed by Mike Cottrell.

Originally performed by Jack Sunderland.

Original Lighting Design by Chloe Stally-Gibson.

Original Sound Design by Chrissy Williams.

Original DJ Consultancy by Gaia Ahuja.

Original Voiceovers by Aaron Phinehas-Peters, Emma Wilkes, Michael Dodds and Tessa Wong.

Biography

Georgie Bailey is an award-winning Playwright, Poet and Producer.

He is a 2020 graduate of Bristol Old Vic Theatre School's MA Dramatic Writing whilst being an alumnus of Soho Theatre, HighTide Theatre and Papatango's respective writer development schemes. Georgie was on attachment to the Oxford Playhouse Playmaker Scheme through 2021 and has worked at numerous venues in facilitating creative writing projects for Young Carers and young people with additional needs.

Georgie has worked with London Playwright's Workshop as their Literary Projects Manager and GHT Southampton as their Lead Young Producer alongside various freelance positions for venues such as Chichester Festival Theatre. He is the Co-Founder of ChewBoy Productions and aims to support early-career creatives of all ages make a career in the arts.

He has won two OffCom awards (*Feel More* & *TETHERED*), a Best of Brighton Fringe Theatre award (*EUAN*), as well as being shortlisted for BOLD Playwrights, Bristol Old Vic Open Session and Longlisted for the Theatre Uncut Award 2021.

Georgie's previous writing credits include: *Tadpoles* (Bristol Old Vic Theatre School), *GORGER* (Oxford Playhouse – Extract), *Drag Me Out* (Hen and Chickens), *EUAN* (Tristan Bates, UK Tour), *Ali – Feel More,* (Lion and Unicorn Theatre), *The Fibster* (Circle Theatre), *These Things That Burn* (Broken Silence Theatre).

Chewboy Productions Biography

ChewBoy Productions are an award-winning multi-arts production company specialising in theatre, film, digital and working with new voices. Established in 2018, they have produced a plethora of multi-disciplinary projects, including their critically acclaimed debut production *EUAN* which enjoyed a UK Tour in 2019 to venues such as Chichester Festival Theatre and Rose Theatre Kingston.

The company creates surrealist work which gives you something to chew on long after you've experienced it; with each project being unique in utilising the skills of creatives from different backgrounds and specialities. ChewBoy champions the development of early-career creatives of any age and the company has worked with over 100 collaborators at the point of publication.

ChewBoy Productions are 2021 associates of the Lion and Unicorn Theatre and digital residents of Living Records Festival. They recently won an OffCOM Short Run award for their critically acclaimed show *TETHERED* and were nominated for the Standing Ovation Award from London Pub Theatres. In 2019, they won the Best of Brighton Fringe Award for their show *EUAN*, alongside picking up multiple 5-star reviews.

Characters

BAZZER   *A primary school disco DJ. Terrified of what they might say next. The definition of someone afraid of the thing they haven't done.*

Heart of gold. A story burning to tell.

VOICES   *A collection of voices throughout the play:*

  MATTY   *YOUNG MATTY*   *BOSS*   *MR BOU*

  MUM   *NURSE*   *DECKS*   *DAD*

NOTE ON THE TEXT

/ indicates an interruption

UPPER CASE doesn't always indicate shouting.

Bold indicates moments where sound design filters in as a second character.

NOTE ON THE SETTING

The play takes place in a variety of locations:

A School Hall (Bazzer's old primary school) // A Hospital Room // A Rooftop in Magaluf.

These could all be portrayed within the same space. The audience might not sit on chairs, they could be plunged back into that nostalgic hole of early-noughties discos.

They could become DJs themselves. Go wild, have fun.

NOTE ON CHARACTER

BAZZER can be played by anyone of any gender, race, sexuality, age or ability.

The other characters should be mainly portrayed through the 'decks' (aka the sound design), and other objects onstage.

Part One

JAMIE VARDY'S HAVIN' A PARTY

BAZZER *stands behind the decks as the audience enter.*

A heavy Electronic DnB set. Glowsticks everywhere.

Maybe an inflatable flamingo somewhere. Maybe sunglasses and a short sleeve flame shirt.
BAZZER *might hide under the decks and re-emerge with new hats etc.*

As the audience enter, **BAZZER** *makes some form of mess onstage (glowsticks, Haribo, whatever's available).*

The house lights gradually fade over the following as a song takes us into…

BAZZER: I'M STANDING ON A ROOFTOP IN MAGALUF.

A PENTHOUSE PARADISE.

SATURATED IN PEOPLE JUST LOOKING FOR A
GOOD TIME.

THEY'RE HERE TO SEE ME, HEAR WHAT I'VE GOT
FOR EM,

HEAR WHAT I'VE GOT IN MY BACK POCKET!

AND I'M READY FOR IT.

AIN'T NOTHING STOPPING ME TODAY!

BAZZER *vibes for a sec. Maybe changes the song.*

BEFORE WE GET STARTED, JUST A FEW HOUSE RULES.

DJ BAZZER'S HOUSE RULES.

LIKE FIGHT CLUB BUT WITH MORE RULES AND, YANO,
NOT LIKE FIGHT CLUB IN THE SLIGHTEST.

THE FIRST RULE OF DJ BAZZER'S HOUSE RULES IS:

PLEASE TURN YOUR MOBILES, TABLETS,
LAPTOPS AND ANY ELECTRONIC DEVICES OFF.

IT MIGHT INTERFERE WITH MY STATE-OF-THE-ART SET-UP.

THE SECOND RULE OF DJ BAZZER'S HOUSE RULES IS:

DON'T TALK ABOUT FIGHT…AAAAAAH!

BAZZER *jokes with the audience.*

NO, REALLY THOUGH, THE SECOND RULE IS:

DON'T TALK ABOUT DJ BAZ, JUST HAVE FUN.

LET LOOSE, DON'T BE A RECLUSE AND MAYBE GRAB A JUICE.

AND THIRD AND FINAL RULE OF DJ BAZZER'S HOUSE RULES IS:

IF YOU NEED TO LEAVE AT ANY POINT, CAN YOU DO IT QUIETLY PLEASE? LIKE A LIZARD

OR…OR…

BAZZER *turns the decks down.*

What're those changing colour lizard things called?

Chamomiles? Jamiroquais?

Someone might shout out, they might not.

Chameleons!

BAZZER *turns the decks back up.*

CHAMELEONS! LEAVE LIKE A CHAMELEON!

I'M JUST QUITE SENSITIVE, SEE.

EMPTY SEATS. DISBANDED GLOWSTICKS.

SO, FINGERS ON LIPS, IF YOU NEED TO LEAVE.

IF YOU REALLY HAVE TO, OK?

LEGGGGOOO!

Sudden change in pace. **Tunes change to primary school DJ vibes.**

An old school late 90's to early-noughties mega mix plays:

Vengaboys. Cha Cha Slide. Busted.

BAZZER: Year 5, please take the floor, it's your moment.

Don't forget to pick up your glowsticks and sweets. 50p offer now on blackjacks and sherbet dib dabs. Gummy bear packs even cheaper. We'll announce the winner of the raffle in half an hour but until then…

BAZZER *reads a note.*

Rose and Hattie, your Mum is outside to collect you, please head to the car park with Mrs Hardman, don't keep her waiting.

Now boys and girls are you ready for a good time?

Let's get that sugar rush a'going, let's get those feet, arms, hands in the air and get ready foooooooooor THE MACARENA!

Time to take it up a gear!

BAZZER *comes out and begins the* **MACARENA.**

It evolves into a DnB remixed version. The worlds of sound are pushing and pulling.

I'M ON A ROOFTOP IN MAGALUF! I SWEAR!

A PENTHOUSE PARADISE.

AND I'M LOOKING AT MY OLD PRIMARY SCHOOL RIVAL

TAKES ME BACK TO THOSE PRIMARY SCHOOL DAYS

AND I GIVE THEM ONE O THESE FROM BEHIND THE DECKS!

BAZZER *holds a middle finger up.*

AND I AM ALIVE! I AM BREATHING! THIS IS LIVING!

The music builds to a crescendo, the decks screaming.

BAZZER *covers their ears.*

DECKS: NO! NO! PLEASE!

BAZZER *slams the laptop lid shut.*

The lights suddenly dim down. **BAZZER** *takes a few long breaths.*

Darkness. Just glowsticks.

Silence.

BAZZER: What I'm about to tell you is entirely non-fiction.

The truth. The whole truth. And nothing but the truth.

It might get tough. You might even cry, you might laugh. Whatever.

Do what ya need to, and I'll do what I need to.

To kill some demons. To live.

Part Two

LOOK AT HIS FACE

Hospital. **Heart rate monitor.** *It punctuates the scene.*

Maybe **BAZZER** *props up the flamingo on the decks. Maybe they don't.*

BAZZER: I'm staring at his face.

Mangled mouth, dented cheeks, blackened eyes. Ghoulish.

Funny word that, ain't it? Ghoulish.

Makes me think of something that's dead, or should be dead,

But isn't quite yet.

I can't see the back of his head. That's where it's worst, apparently.

But I dunno. Can't see it. Just see this face.

This gaunt, paper white face. Ghoulish.

He's got this tube? Thing? Coming out his mouth, it's really big
and it's attached to some machine that's making these weird
like HUUUURH noises? And it's freaking me out a bit, to be
honest, cus...

It looks bad. Really, really quite bad.

And I'm thinking...

He's too young to be looking like this.

And I think about what if I was in his position.

Looking like that. All...ghoulish.

Beat.

Through the following, the heart rate monitor **could quicken** *with* **BAZZER***'s
anxiety.*

BAZZER: I think about playing some music?

Liven the place up a bit, make it feel a bit less…bleak.

Maybe it'll wake him up, get him out of this thing he's got himself into,

But I look around and it seems a bit, like, insensitive?

There's an old geeza laid up in the bed opposite, and he's in one too, and then *that* gets me thinking:

Do people still shit in a coma? Do they piss? Do they just…do it on themselves? It's got me thinking about all these things, and my mind it's like, it's just *going* right? Like, like you know when you're about to fall asleep, yeah, and you just kinda start thinking about one little thing, yeah? And then the little thing snowballs and become a bigger thing and then suddenly you're thinking about the things that you don't really *need* to be thinking about right now but your brain is suddenly like – if you don't think about this right now then you ain't ever gonna think again? Like at all? Like like like like like if –

Beat.

BAZZER *tunes back into the* ***heart rate monitor****.*

I channel back into the thing I've come here to do.

And I think about how this is gonna be a very long night.

Part Three

READY UP FOR SCHOOL, SKIPPER!

The school bell rings.

It's ten years later.

BAZZER *gets changed, quickly. Caretaker clothes. Grabs a broom.*

Sweeps the floors, tidies up the mess they made earlier in Part One.

BAZZER *should improv with the audience, asking if certain things are theirs, playing games with them, slagging off the mess before…*

BAZZER: Kids these days, they don't half make a mess, do they?

And who's the one that has to tidy up after 'em?

Got me thinkin' like, was it always this way?

At what point did I become the tidier of the tidy-less?

BAZZER *continues tidying.*

BAZZER: I'm thirty-five. I'm sweepin' up classrooms in my old Primary School.

Givin' back to the community, yano.

Also help 'em out with the discos. They love 'em, and to be fair, so do I.

Here, tonight is the Year 6 Leavers' Disco: the event of the year.

Each time it comes round I get a lil flutter in my stomach. I just get so GASSED! And this year, I've got a corker of a setlist lined up:

Venga Boys | Atomic Kitten | Leona Lewis *(for the end of the night when we're being reflective)* | Girls Aloud | Dexys Midnight Runners just to name a bloody FEW!

It's gonna go off. It's gonna go off big time.

And I am off my NUT with excitement.

And no, it won't be any of their Jessie J, 1975, Ed Sheeran shit.

It's gonna be real music. Real, energy ridden, beat stricken, banger qualified music. And ain't no one's gonna tell me anything different.

I'm thirty-five! I think I know a thing or two about MUSIC.

Like, we all remember the discos, right? The rite of passage into adulthood. Secrets shared, shapes thrown, songs sung till you had a sore throat. And I think, the way I remember them is probably very different to you. Or you. Or you, even.

Cus we all remember things differently, right? Two people's version of one story are always butting heads, but it's about which one is true to *you*, yeah?

Goes back to sweeping. Notices some dominoes on the floor.

They pick one up, inspecting it. They place one down, beginning the formation.

BAZZER: I love games. Always have. Always will.

Love playing them. Love being part of them.

Love making up new ones.

Do you like games? Do you wanna play one? With me?

I won't patronise you, do you wanna play or not?

Take this. Go on.

BAZZER *hands the domino to an audience member.*

Pop it down right here.

BAZZER *encourages the person to place the domino in a specific place.*

See! Wasn't that fun. Aren't we having fun? Can I get an "oh yeah!"

"OH YEAH!"

Ok, ok, take a seat, thanks.

They get another domino out, placing it next to the last one.

It's nice, you all joining me.

Nice to have company, ain't it?

So that you don't get swept up in all the chatter…the noise inside the ol head. Things you shoulda said. Things said to you.

Bouncing around like the ghost of a kangaroo.

Smacking. Punching. Clawing with everything it has.

Nice to have company, to stop those…those…

Beat.

Or…are you here to judge me? Not listen, but judge?

Is this my reckoning? Because people remember things differently, ok, not everything that one person says is exactly how things happened. How they panned out, ok. People lie. So, I want you to remember that if nothing else out of all this. So, think on that, and *then,* and *then…*

Stares at the dominoes a while. Goes back to sweeping, noticeably faster. Erratic.

BAZZER: Did you know that music helps plants grow faster?

Thas why I like playing it for the kids, maybe they'll be giants. The superhumans of Brigdale school…And and, and did you know, right, listen, did you know that none of the Beatles could read music? Imagine that! Being arguably the most prolific band of ALL time and not being able to-to-to-

Martin Block was the first ever *Radio* DJ

But a kid called Ray Newby did it all first as a laugh in 1909

Before the term DJ even existed

DJ Stands for Disc Jockey.

And, last, last one for ya,

Music helps people with brain injuries recall personal memories.

BAZZER *breathes deeply.*

I'm not awful, I'm not a horrible person. I promise you that.

Because the thing is, right –

School bell.

Part Four

BAZZER *puts on some sunglasses again. Resumes position behind the decks.*

BAZZER *plays* **Superman by Black Lace** *or the* **Cha Cha Slide** *by* **DJ Casper**. *Something which the audience recognise and could maybe dance along to.*

GALILEO: Now, Year Five, let's play a little game – How much can you Tango for a can of Tango?! Best dance move gets a free can of Tango!

> **BAZZER** *could be dancing in the space, as if* **GALILEO** *is controlling the decks.*
>
> *Or,* **BAZZER** *could dance with the audience, getting them up.*

ROBBIE – NO KISSING.

CHARLOTTE – NO HANDSTANDS, YOU KNOW YOU GET HEADACHES FROM HANDSTANDS.

BARRY – STOP ACTING LIKE A BIG MAN, WE KNOW YOU'RE NOT A BIG MAN!

BAZZER: It all started in school.

Got my first taste of the beats at the Year Five disco.

I'd been to school discos, birthday parties, the works, but,

THIS guy – Galileo. He was tearing the place up.

Like a musical magician, taking us on a magical music tour.

He controlled the room like an Aircraft Marshal bringing us in to land.

The star in my eyes. The centre of the Universe.

Galileo.

Proper *sound* geeza.

And ya see, at the discos, you'd always have the groups, right?

You had your cool kids, always at the back, bopping their heads every now and then to a beat like this.

Then you had your inbetweeners, the ones who were shy, but get enough haribo in their veins and they'd be OFF. Knee sliding, conga lining, cha cha sliding all over the place.

And then you had your rubber eaters. You know the ones, the ones who'd pick their noses with pencils. The ones who'd have this unexplainable smell. The ones with questionable shirts on.

But Galileo, see, he had this way of bringing them all together, breaking down those barriers.

Bringing pure bliss to the primary school discos.

Bringing the best times out in all of us.

But, well, ya see, it was also a time of worry, amongst all the happiness and joy. It was a time of dread, for little old Barry.

When I were in year five, I got my first rival.

Matty Bovril. Galileo's Son.

Maybe an image of **MATTY** *could appear, or he could be the inflatable flamingo.*

MATTY *could be portrayed through the orange hat.*

One of the cool-kid-gang through and through.

Matty was the best at everything.

Good at sport // Good at drama shit // And most importantly

Good at music.

The best at music, apparently.

I thought he were shit! Proper shit. But everyone loved him.

And so, he's out there, right now, doing big gigs in London; underground caves, underage drinking raves, secret dens where he can spout off all his crap, leaving the proper talent (me) to die in the dark. To die in the school halls of years gone by.

AND he'd always wear this stupid orange hat.

BAZZER *has the hat.*

He thought it was cool but he looked like a knob.

The decks malfunction. The music is quieter now: **OUTKAST – HEY YA.**

BAZZER *reverts to their younger self.*

YOUNG MATTY*'s voice comes through:*

YOUNG MATTY: What is this?

BAZZER: It's Outkast.

YOUNG MATTY: Hey Ya is it?

BAZZER: It's my favourite song.

YOUNG MATTY: It's mine too!

BAZZER: It was mine first.

YOUNG MATTY: So you wanna be a DJ, yeah? My Dad's a DJ!

BAZZER: Wait, wait…he didn't sound like this.

BAZZER *changes the decks.*

YOUNG MATTY: So you wanna be a DJ, yeah?

BAZZER: Better.

YOUNG MATTY: My Dad's a DJ!

BAZZER: Yeah, a rubbish one.

YOUNG MATTY: Why you copying my Dad?

BAZZER: Your Dad copied me.

YOUNG MATTY: My Dad doesn't copy people.

BAZZER: *My* Dad could beat *your* Dad in a fight.

YOUNG MATTY: DJing is for cool people.

BAZZER: I'm cool enough to DJ.

YOUNG MATTY: No you're not.

BAZZER: Am.

YOUNG MATTY: Not.

BAZZER: AM!

YOUNG MATTY: NOT!

BAZZER: I'M COOLER THAN YOU!

YOUNG MATTY: Why you being so loud?

BAZZER: Why you being a NOOB?

YOUNG MATTY: DJing sounds cool.

BAZZER: Don't you dare.

YOUNG MATTY: I might give it a go.

BAZZER: DON'T YOU DARE

YOUNG MATTY: Wish me / luck.

> **BAZZER** *shuts the laptop lid.*

BAZZER: You ever play over stuff back in your head.

The crucial moments in life // The ones that made all the difference // The fork in the crossroads // The conversations where you think of what you shoulda said after // Those specific specks in time

And wished you'd caved their fucking skull in?

The school bell rings, again.

> **BAZZER** *heads back round to the decks,* ***plays one of*** **MATTY***'s* ***bangers.***

22

Part Five

BACK ONCE AGAIN TO THE MAGALUF MASTER

BAZZER *in Magaluf regalia again.*

BAZZER: I'm twenty-two.

I'm on a rooftop in Magaluf having a mediocre time.

There's sun rays burning my skin cus Mum said the factor thirty would be fine and it isn't cus look at it. I'm a bloody lobster.

This random guy in a Metallica t-shirt comes up to me and asks "are you not hot mate" and I say of course I am Steven, it's 30 degrees in Magaluf, you tit. And Metallica aren't even that good. They have like what, three good songs? Two at the most? And did you know –

STEVEN*'s gone.*

I'm pretty pissed. I'm seeing double, a bit.

And this rooftop is weird. I don't know anyone and…

I'm kinda blending in?

No one's really noticing me. Not since Metalhead Steven left.

And I'm not sure…I don't know how to talk to anyone.

The sun is beating down on my forehead like a bloodsucking maggot.

My drink is too sugary, I'm feeling buzzed but not in a nice way.

And I get this…rising feeling? In my chest? Almost like someone's pushing a boulder up my throat and I'm…

BAZZER *stares ahead, breathing heavily.*

I head to the smoking area to have a cig,

As they always say when you're feeling bad, do something that makes you feel worse, right?

BAZZER *might mime a ciggie. They might use a domino, who knows.*

It's this quiet little smoking area behind where the party is kicking off.

And no one's here. Apart from this random guy in a Metallica t-shirt.

It's the middle of a big set, apparently.

But all it is really, to you and me, is a BTEC kinda gig.

No one of real value.

So, the smoking area, albeit shit, is the place to be, right now. For me.

And I look up from the floor, after trying to channel my energy into something that isn't this sense of impending doom to see him there.

Matty fucking Bovril. Wearing that shitty orange hat.

Laughing, hitting people on the shoulder, like some Adonis sent from above. And I have this wave of…something. Can't put my finger on what that something is, but it's there.

He clocks eyes with me. Half recognising, half avoiding for now.

And that riles this feeling up even more.

And then he says something dumb like "one-minute *guys*" and before I know it, he's…he's…

Before I know it, we're…

BAZZER *tries to console themselves.*

BAZZER: Did you know, that musicians have the shortest life span of anyone?

Did you know that there's a national Disc Jockey day? January 20th.

Did you know that jealousy is the only emotion we can't put into words?

We can't describe it. Think about it. How would you describe jealousy?

And did you know –

The decks kick into action on their own.

BOSS: Excuse me, Baz? Could I have a word?

BAZZER: Um. Not right now / sorry –

BOSS: It'll only take a moment.

BAZZER: But not this / moment.

BOSS: I need to speak with / you.

BAZZER: I didn't / do it.

BOSS: Baz.

BAZZER: I DIDN'T / DO IT!

BOSS: IN HERE. NOW.

   School bell. Loud, harsh.

Part Six

INTO THE HEART OF THE HEADMASTER'S OFFICE

BAZZER *is sat sheepishly, still thirty-five.*

BAZZER: Sorry, I'm not following.

BOSS: We've been approached by someone new.

BAZZER: Did I do something wrong?

BOSS: You've been doing this for over ten years now, Barry. Your songs are getting a bit…

BAZZER: A bit?

BOSS: Past it, I'm afraid.

BAZZER: Past it.

BOSS: This new DJ has got all the tracks the kids are loving these days. Stormy, Duolipo, Lizzy –

BAZZER: It's all shit!

BOSS: I fear you're a bit stuck in the past, Barry.

BAZZER: Am not.

BOSS: I think it's good for you to spread those wings!

BAZZER: I'm not a bird.

BOSS: New ventures are awaiting you!

Beat.

BAZZER: So I'm…

BOSS: So you're…

BAZZER: I'm leaving?

BOSS: If that's ok with you!

BAZZER: No, no that's, that's that's…that's fine that's –

BOSS: Of course, you can keep your caretaking position, if you so wish.

The resident sweeper, *Barry*!

BAZZER: Who's taking over?

BOSS: Confidential.

BAZZER: Who's taking over?

BOSS: Confidential my boy!

BAZZER: WHO'S TAKING OVER?

BOSS: Confidential my / boy –

BAZZER *is back to the audience.*

BAZZER: WHAT THE FUCK IS THIS ALL ABOUT?

I'VE BEEN A DEDICATED MEMBER OF THIS TEAM FOR
TEN YEARS AS THE IN-HOUSE DJ AND NOW THEY JUST
WANNA SLING ME OUT MY SHITTING ARSE LIKE SOME
SORT OF DISCARDED MUPPET PUPPET THE FUCKING –

BAZZER *could kick the decks, they could hurt their foot.*

As they (potentially) kick, the decks spit out an **underscore for memories.**

BAZZER: I'm ten years old.

I get a set of plastic DJ decks from Mum for Christmas.

I stay up all night pretending to be Fat Boy Slim, Carl Cox,
Romanthony, shit, even Craig bloody *David*. I'm wearing hats,
headphones, puffing on a candy stick. I'm playing Spice Girls through
my disc Walkman. I'm flicking the lights on and off and Mum howls
at me to stop doing that or I'll blow the bulbs.

MUM: STOP DOING THAT, YOU'LL BLOW THE BLOODY
BULBS!

BAZZER: I'm ten years old and I'm having the time of my fucking life.

I'm fourteen years old and I tell everyone about my dream. My music teacher at school, Mr Bouillard, ain't convinced, cus he's into the more classical renaissance-esque vibes of the olden days. He always says to me, he says:

MR BOU: YOU WANT TO PICK UP A REAL INSTRUMENT RATHER THAN WASTING ALL YOUR POTENTIAL ON A LITTLE BOYS' GAME.

BAZZER: But I *am* a little boy, so I tell him where to stick it, and that year I win second place at the secondary school talent contest: Brigdale's Got Talent. Second place is, in some cases, better than first. A robbed win. I'm eighteen years old.

I'm walking down the high street.

I see a promoter outside a new bar and I ask her if they're looking for any music support. Techies. Stagehands. DJ's, maybe.

She laughs at me, but thinks I've got a bit of '*swag*' as she put it,

PROMO: YOU'RE QUITE COOL MATE…

BAZZER: So I'm there the next night on the decks. And it goes well, and someone there gives me a card and then I'm calling them up, and they're talking about a collab, and I think it's all going good and then and then and then…

They ask me for an investment.

I'm twenty-two and I'm on a rooftop in Magaluf, wondering where it all went wrong for me to be having a panic attack in front of a group of strangers, watching other people do what I wanna do and be shit at it.

Beat.

So, now, I'm thirty-five. And the crumb of it all I had left is being slowly nibbled away at by some little ratty fucking twat with –

BOSS: CONFIDENTIAL, MY BOY!

BAZZER *returns to position.* ***The underscore is cut short.***

BAZZER: I'm still doing Year 6 Leavers' Disco tonight.

BOSS: Now, Barry –

BAZZER: You promised! I always get Leavers' Disco!

BOSS: We think it's / best if

BAZZER: No no no no NO You promised.

BOSS: But I'm not sure the Year 6's want your 'tunes' anymore, Barry –

BAZZER: I have to do it.

Beat.

I have to do it because it's the only time I get to feel like I'm actually contributing something // everyone remembers the first song that got them bopping at the Year 6 prom // everyone remembers the sugar-rush-hand-holding and the not-quite-understood fear of the future that is surging to the pit of the stomach // I'm the one to play those songs to make them know… it'll all be ok // Someday // Someday where they don't have to be jealous of another…

Beat.

Matty.

BOSS: Hm?

BAZZER: Matty Bovril. Is this because of Matty?

His Dad used to do the DJ sets here. Galileo Bovril.

If that *was* his real name.

BOSS: Matty! No, nothing about Matty, God no.

He was a big fan of that Outkast song, wasn't he? Hey You!

BAZZER: Because it really didn't happen how you might think.

BOSS: Matty's only just woken up, Barry.

Beat.

We just think it's time to get some new blood on our disco dancefloor!

Think about my offer, hm? The resident caretaker!

BAZZER: He's woken up?

BOSS: Hm?

BAZZER: Matty. He's woken up? Are you… is this…

BAZZER *begins to feel uneasy.*

BOSS: Ok, Baz, it's ok. Take it easy, hm?

You can still do the Leavers' Disco tonight, how about that? You do it!

One final gig, hm?

BAZZER *stares into space. Long. The world seems to tunnel in.*

Part Seven

DON'T HUG ME I'M TERRIFIED

BAZZER *puts on a song*. It could be ***Threnody for the Victims of Hiroshima***.

It might not be as intense as that…

They place dominos around the space. It takes a long, long time. Focussed.

When they're finished…

BAZZER: I'm twenty-two.

> I'm stood on a rooftop in Magaluf, in the smoking area.
>
> And Matty Bovril is there, chewing my ear off,
>
> Trying to one-up me constantly. In his stupid little orange hat.
>
> He's asking me questions about what I'm up to
>
> And I don't tell him about the investment that went wrong at eighteen,
>
> I don't tell him about the DJ battle I was laughed out of.
>
> I don't tell him about the growing sense that what I'm doing isn't good enough because that's *exactly* what he wants to hear.
>
> He wants to know how badly I'm doing so he can rub it in my face and I won't give him that pleasure.
>
> He's going on about this gig he's doing next week in Ibiza, and the set he's got coming up today. And he's talking about –

MATTY: When the beats are just hitting *right* and you know they're hitting *right*, and you're looking out over the arena, and everyone's just *vibing*, you know? You know when you get that. When you get that *feeling*? That's what it's all about, *right*?

BAZZER: The sun is slugging away at my face, and I can feel it reaching its way down my throat. Like it might never let my skin go.

The distant echoes of people living for life are ricocheting between my ears and I feel like they're talking about me.

My hand grips onto this shitty mojito tighter

And I feel like a cretin.

My head is pounding, my chest is locked, ready to implode if I give it half a chance and my legs feel like they're gonna collapse.

I'm thinking about music facts to calm me down and I think about how stupid it is that I have to resort to music facts to calm me down.

And today, on this blistering day at twenty-two in Magaluf…

they don't work.

I'm tuning Matty out but giving a few nods like a nodding dog with an iron deficiency.

And then as I'm tuning out, I'm tuning into these voices.

These ghosts. These…ghouls. And they start to sound familiar.

They blend, they transform, they pollute the noise.

words that have been said. Words that haven't yet.

Smashing into my brain like a group of wrecking balls into a wall.

Over the following, **the music grows in pace and volume.**

The voices could clash with one another.

MR BOU: YOU WANT TO PICK UP A REAL INSTRUMENT, RATHER THAN WASTING ALL YOUR POTENTIAL ON A LITTLE BOYS GAME.

BOSS: CONFIDENTIAL, MY BOY.

BAZZER: It's not

DAD: CAN'T YOU GET A CHEAPER HOBBY?

BAZZER: It's not a hobby

BOSS: ANY HOBBIES?

BAZZER: IT'S NOT A HOBBY.

MATTY: I never said it was.

MR BOU: FIND SOMETHING YOU'RE BETTER AT.

MUM: YOU'LL BLOW THE ELECTRICS OUT.

BOSS: SOMEONE NEW SOMEONE FRESH.

MUM: IT'LL COST ME MONEY.

DECKS: CAN YOU STOP SPOUTING MUSIC FACTS FOR ONE SECOND?

DECKS: YOU DON'T REALLY WANT TO DO THIS.

DECKS: DO YOU REALLY WANT TO DO THIS?

DECKS: COME ON NOW, GIVE IT UP.

DECKS: GIVE IT UP.

DECKS: GIVE IT UP.

DECKS: GIVE IT UP.

DECKS: GIVE IT UP.

DECKS: GIVE IT UP.

DECKS: GIVE IT UP.

MATTY: YOU'RE NOT AS GOOD AS ME ANYWAY!

BAZZER: You don't even know.

MATTY: YOU'RE NOT GOOD ENOUGH!

BAZZER: AND *THEN* HE FUCKING LAUGHS AT ME

MATTY: C'MON MATE, WE CAN'T ALL BE BRILLIANT **CAN WE!**

BAZZER: AND I LAUNCH AT HIM, AND I GRAB HIM AND HE'S THERE ON THE EDGE AND I JUST –

MATTY: NO! NO!

PLEASE!

BAZZER *pushes the dominoes over. It could be quiet, controlled destruction, with one Domino falling off a higher area. It could be hideously charged and chaotic. Whatever feels right for your* **BAZZER.**

Once they're finished, they hold the orange hat.

A hollow kind of silence.

Part Eight

THE EYE OF THE BEHOLDER

Hospital. **Life support machine beeping.**

BAZZER *is stood at the door.*

BAZZER: I'm thirty-five. I'm thinking about the last time I was here.

Twenty-two. They had to fly him from Magaluf back to England.

I came late at night so no one would be around. Sat there all night trying to…say something.

And here I am, again now. To do what I couldn't do back then.

Beat.

I'm stood at the door of his hospital room.

Wondering if that old guy who was in a coma has died, or shat himself, or pissed all over himself. And I wonder how many of those Matty's done since I was last here. I hold his orange hat in my hand.

And then, and then…

BAZZER *doesn't describe how they feel for the first time. They just feel it.*

BAZZER: I'm thinking what this means for me if he remembers?

Like, what if he knows? Will he tell everyone?

Or, is it worse if he doesn't? Do I have to tell him? And then I think…

What if he's not the person I remember?

And what if…

What if I haven't remembered it right?

Did I actually…could I actually have…*(done that?)*

Monaco's Army is smaller than its Military Orchestra // Prince played twenty-seven instruments on his debut album // some people feel nothing towards // some people with brain injuries can remember –

NURSE: You alright, love?

BAZZER: I bolt into the room and close the door behind me. And… he's there.

    MATTY *could be represented by the flamingo, or even just the decks.*

    His eyes are blank. They trace my body from head to toe.

    Not a flicker. Not a whisper even of the life they used to have.

    Hiiii mate. Long-time no see!

    Nothing.

    You ok? How're you…how's…

    He starts shaking his head. He looks out the window.

    He breathes heavily, like Darth Vader if Darth Vader had just woken up from a twelve-year coma.

    Nice long sleep you had! Hah. Must be well rested.

    His chest rises and falls even quicker now.

    I'm doing a gig at the primary school tonight.

    Year 6 Leavers' Disco. Remember those? Hah.

    My last one. Yeah. Don't really know what I'll do after –

    His face turns to look at me. He's squinting. Looking.

    And he has that look of disgust on his face that he always used to have. In the playground. At the discos. Like I'm somehow…*worse.*

    And now…I want him to remember me.

    I don't care what it'll mean, I don't care what'll happen.

    I need him to remember me.

    BAZZER *heads to decks, puts on* **HEY YA *by* OUTKAST**.

BAZZER *tries to get him to remember. Really badly.*

BAZZER: WHY CAN'T YOU REMEMBER!

HERE, HERE'S YOUR HAT, DOES THAT HELP? DOES IT?

I'M BAZZER.

WE USED TO KNOW EACH OTHER, DIDN'T WE?

WE USED TO PLAY TOP TRUMPS? WE STAYED IN A TENT TOGETHER ON THE YEAR 4 CAMPING TRIP. STAYED UP ALL NIGHT TALKING ABOUT AND LISTENING TO AND, AND...

BAZZER.

WHAT DO YOU WANT ME TO SAY? THAT I'M SORRY? IS THAT WHAT YOU WANT? SPEAK TO ME MATTY FOR FUCK SAKE!

In broken speech, **MATTY***'s voice:*

MATTY: B-a...zzzzz-err.

Beat.

B-azzer.

Beat.

H...eeeey y-y-y...yaaaaa.

Reverts to **MATTY***'s younger voice.*

HEEEEY YAAAAAA!

BAZZER: Matty...I –

MATTY: I'm proud of you.

BAZZER: What? No you're...you're meant to be –

MATTY: I miss you. Where've you been all these / years

BAZZER: You're not meant to be like this.

YOU'RE NOT MEANT TO BE LIKE THIS.

YOU'RE NOT…THIS ISN'T THE VERSION THAT I –

MATTY: Don't you remember?

Beat.

Don't you remember how it used to be?

*The decks play an echoed version of **Hey Ya! by Outkast.***

BAZZER: No, no no no this isn't…it's not –

BAZZER *puts on a track. The beginning of his **YEAR 6 DISCO SETLIST.***

Part Nine

THE WHIMPER

BAZZER *frantically gets the stage ready, maybe leaving it in more of a state than it already was to begin with. They get changed into their Year 6 Disco outfit.*

They take their place behind the decks.

A mega mix of early noughties bangers should play under the following sequence. It should be different to the one at the top of the play.

This is **BAZZER***'s final purge. The final disco.*

BAZZER *tries to maintain their anxiety through the decks.*

The following doesn't have to be shouted.

BAZZER: All having a good time? Can I get an 'oh yeah!'

OH YEAH! Ok, let's turn this up a notch Year 6…

BAZZER *moves the mega mix on. Trying to get things going. Uncomfortable.*

THIS IS THE FINAL BIT OF THE NIGHT! IF YOU HAVEN'T GOT UP AND DANCED YET, GET DANCING!

FREE CAN OF TANGO FOR THE BEST TANGO AND… AND…

BAZZER *throws out glowsticks, gets amongst the crowd.*

KAYLEIGH – REMEMBER TO TAKE SOME IBUPROFEN IF YOUR SHINS START TO HURT

TOBY – KEEP AWAY FROM THE HARIBO AND SUGARY DRINKS, YOU KNOW YOU SHOULDN'T BE HAVING THEM

MATTY – MATTY – MATTY – please…don't…*(die)*

BAZZER *moves the mega mix on.*

IT'S THE YEAR 6 LEAVERS' DISCO // I'M HAVING THE TIME OF MY LIFE // ALL THE KIDS ARE ON A SUGAR

RUSH // THERE'S SOME KINDA FRUIT PUNCH THAT
THEY'RE PRETENDING IS BOOZE // CAUGHT IT OFF
THEIR PARENTS LIKE A VIRUS // A SICKNESS // A
DISEASE // AND I'M LOOKIN' AT ALL THESE KIDS AND
// AND I CAN KINDA SEE THEIR FUTURES HANGING IN
THE BALANCE // LIKE THAT BIT IN DONNIE DARKO //
SEEING THEIR SPIRITS LEAVE EM // KNOWING WHAT
COMES NEXT IS…THIS // A SHADE OF ME // LOOKING
LIKE THIS // AND I CAN'T STOP THINKING ABOUT
WHAT THE FUTURE MEANS // AND WHAT A GOOD
FUTURE MEANS // AND WHAT IS SUPPOSED TO BE OUT
THERE FOR US.

THERE'S A KID BEING SICK IN THE CORNER.

THERE'S TWO BEST FRIENDS CRYING ON SHOULDERS

CUS OF THE DIFFERENT SCHOOLS THEY'RE GOING TO.

THERE'S A KID WHO LOOKS LIKE

Dream-like state. Soft focus.

He looks like

There's a kid who looks like Matty.

Who's come over to the ones crying.

And he's patting them on the back and he's

He's // It'll all be alright, is what he's saying and he's

BAZZER *is flailing.*

ARE WE ALL HAVING A GOOD TIME?

WE'RE ALL HAVING FUUUUUUN AIN'T WE?

WE'RE ALL HAVING // AND WE'RE NOT // WE'RE NOT,

NO, WE'RE NOT // NOT THINKING ABOUT HOW WE

The decks begin to malfunction. **BAZZER** *could be left just on mic.*

ABOUT HOW WE MISREMEMBER EVENTS IN OUR LIVES

ABOUT HOW WE FORGET WHAT PEOPLE DID FOR US

ABOUT HOW THE FUTURE IS THE MOST TERRIFYING THING

ABOUT HOW IT'S EASY TO THINK OF DEATH AS A FRIEND

ABOUT HOW IT'S EASY TO THINK THAT WAY

ABOUT HOW THIS MIGHT BE THE LAST THING I DO

ABOUT HOW DJ'ING AT MY OLD PRIMARY SCHOOL IS THE ONLY THING THAT MAKES ME FEEL CLOSER TO HIM

ABOUT HOW IT MAKES ME REMEMBER IT RIGHT

ABOUT HOW WE WERE BEST FRIENDS

ABOUT HOW HE WAS THE BEST

ABOUT HOW HE WAS SUPPORTIVE

ABOUT HOW HE WAS LIKE THE BROTHER I NEVER…

ABOUT HOW THINGS REALLY WERE

ABOUT HOW I'M // ABOUT HOW

BAZZER *puts* **MATTY**'*s hat on.*

ABOUT HOW THIS IS DEDICATED TO MY BEST FRIEND

MATTY BOVRIL.

The decks malfunction, they suddenly cut out. Broken. **The noise dissipates, evaporates into the air.** **BAZZER** *is left. Sans anything.*

Part Ten

THESES FACES LOOK LIKE OURS

BAZZER: I…I look around the hall. A vacant black hole. A void of what once was.

The kids have all gone home. All picked up by a family who cares.

The lingering ghost of sweat clings to the blue brick, that unexplainable smell of a kid's party. And I look around at this room, taking it in for one last time. Thinking of the years spent here, the days I'll never get back.

Thinking about the sweeping up of classrooms.

About the things burrowed away in the now empty corridors, the cupboards. Thinking about the time left.

Thinking about how loneliness is a real, living, breathing thing.

And like some kinda magic trick, this kid appears. Rabbit from a hat.

And it's the Matty lookalike from earlier.

And he's staring at me, from across the hall.

BAZZER does a sheepish wave.

*Realises the decks are broken. To tell this part, **BAZZER** either turns on a Bluetooth speaker, or gives the final page of script from the technician, or lost property box, to an audience member.*

Bringing this metaphorical, abstract world into reality.

MATTY: When I grow up, I wanna be a DJ, just like you Baz!

BAZZER: You don't wanna be like me.

MATTY: You didn't really push him though!

BAZZER: I wish I had.

MATTY: You couldn't do that to someone!

BAZZER: I could've done to him.

MATTY: No! He was your best friend. And only a little better at DJing!

BAZZER: Anyone can be a DJ. Even you.

MATTY: Even me?

BAZZER: Especially you.

MATTY: Keep at it!

BAZZER: Keep at what?

MATTY: Being who you want to be. Not who they say you should be.

BAZZER: Keep at it.

> **BAZZER** *takes off the orange cap. Holds it out.*

This was a friend of mine's once. Maybe it'll do you some good.

MATTY: Thanks Baz!

BAZZER: And he races off down the hall, after his mate comes through the door to hurry him along. His best mate, maybe.

Maybe that's me…from time gone by.

Before he leaves, he pivots like an NBA player.

And a wave from his tiny hand barely grown.

A hand that's barely felt the world at all.

And in that wave, a knowing, in me, growing, I think.

That maybe everything I am right now, is enough.

It has to be enough. For me.

> **BAZZER** *waves down the hall at* **MATTY**. ***The clock ticks and grows louder.***

Right?

END.

Georgie Bailey

Tethered

(Or, The Adventures of the Adequately Excited People)

A new play from ChewBoy Productions

George and Hal are putting on a play. They're playing Moins and Sans. George needs it to be perfect. Hal's fallen out of love with it.

As the pair traverse through their madcap story of party hats, balloonies and mysterious messages, the actors are forced to question many things. Like, how far would we go to keep ourselves sane when trapped in one place for too long? How much do we rely on each other? And how do you pronounce Moins?

TETHERED is an award-winning surreal comedy from the critically acclaimed ChewBoy Productions, exploring hope, loss, and dependence, following a successful run at the Lion and Unicorn Theatre where the company are Associate Artists.

Salamander Street

PLAYS

Acknowledgements

TETHERED was originally performed at the Lion and Unicorn Theatre, Kentish Town in July 2021.

Originally directed by Lucy Betts.

Originally performed by Hal Darling & Georgie Bailey.

Original Assistant Director: Selwin Hulme-Teague.

Characters

SANS / HAL

MOINS / GEORGE

NOTES

The characters should be tethered together – either with rope, chain, or other material.

All stage directions, when next to a character's name, are spoken.

In its first production, the play was staged with the set being a rehearsal room. Party hats, rope, balloons. The works. There was a working tech desk on stage.

The characters are gender neutral and can be played by any actor of any ethnicity, gender or age.

The setting is left ambiguous, and we encourage different interpretations for both the audience and each unique production.

There are two worlds: the play within the play (SANS & MOINS) and the rehearsal room (GEORGE & HAL). These two worlds should be defined to begin with, and then blur.

All improvised moments have been labelled, but it's encouraged to be played in response to the performer's strengths, and their shared interests to present an honest relationship.

In the original production at the Lion and Unicorn in 2021, we utilised a load of different acting styles such as Laurel and Hardy, EastEnders, Oliver!, Children's TV Presenters, Epic Theatre / Shakespearean and GSCE Drama to name a few in the play within the play. Each company should find their own styles. (And mainly, have fun!)

A | THE PRE-SET.

Two actors, **GEORGE** *and* **HAL**, *stand onstage.*

They are busy. **GEORGE** *plays music.* **GEORGE** *tries to convince* **HAL** *they should use the music choices he's found in the play for specific moments.*

HAL'*s not having it. It builds into a heated conversation, ending in a funny line (change every night) in response to the conversation.*

HAL: Shall we just start.

GEORGE: Yeah.

> **GEORGE** *hits play on the tech desk, music kicks in.*

> *The pair dance a dance which celebrates the history of theatre, before coming round…*

SANS: SANS *enters the space.*

MOINS: MOINS *enters the space.*

HAL: Mwans?

GEORGE: Yeah.

HAL: Not Moynes?

MOINS: *They are*

BOTH: *tethered*

MOINS: *together.*

SANS: *The rope is exactly 2m in length.*

MOINS: *Sans and Mwans take up some acting positions.*

BOTH: *They are serious actors. This is a serious play.*

SANS: *They begin the search for the start of the story.*

MOINS: *They begin the search for the start of the story.*

BOTH: *They begin the search for the start of the story.*

HAL: Or whatever was on the marketing blurb synopsis thingy!

The play within the play BREAKS. The lights snap.

GEORGE *turns the music off.*

GEORGE: Look, if you're not going to take this seriously, there's no point in doing it is there?

HAL: I'm just not sure it fits with the rest of the…

GEORGE: If you half arse it, we'll just look silly. But if you go for it, really go for it then maybe we could look really cool.

HAL: Really cool? We're galloping like Mr Tumnus for fuck sake.

GEORGE: I'm trying really hard here, Hal.

Beat.

HAL: I'm sorry.

GEORGE: I don't need you to be sorry, I just…shall we just give it a go?

HAL: Ok. Yeah, sure. Ready?

GEORGE: Ready.

BACK IN:

MOINS: SANS *and* **MOINS** *notice some strange looking onlookers.*

SANS: *They are noticeably afraid,*

MOINS: *But also adequately intrigued.*

SANS: Who will flip my lucky flipper?

MOINS: Their lucky flipper is very flippable.

SANS: We need a flipper!

MOINS: A flipper is what we need!

SANS: Half of our story is held by Heads.

MOINS: The other held by Tails.

SANS: The face that is flipped…

MOINS: Determines our order of proceedings, how we tell you what we need to. **MOINS** *notices SOMEONE in the crowd.*

SANS: *They approach like a rabid animal, with prey in their sights.*

MOINS: *(To an audience member.)* You will be our flipper! Our caller and our flipper!

SANS: Our flapper!

MOINS: Our killer!

HAL: That's not in the script.

MOINS: I thought we were doing a funny word thing.

HAL: Are we improvising now?

MOINS: Try it, it's fun, our *killer*!

HAL: What?

SANS: You said they were a killer. We don't know if they're a killer.

MOINS: Are they a killer? Are you / a killer?

HAL: And where do we go from here?

GEORGE: Woah, ok.

Lights snap out.

HAL: What?

GEORGE: You interrupted me.

HAL: It was going on too long, you were too slow.

GEORGE: "YoU wErE tOo SlOw!"

HAL: "YOU WERE TOO SLOW"

GEORGE: "YoU wErE tOo SlOw!"

HAL: "YOU WERE TOO SLOOOOOOOW"

This goes on for a while until…

HAL: *GEORGE was too slow.*

> **GEORGE** *stops, offended.*

Oh what, you going to get offended now?

It's improv, baby!

GEORGE: Yeah well maybe I don't wanna improv anymore, yeah? Maybe I'm not as good as I thought I was at it.

IMPROVISATION ONE:

The characters talk about whether they should or shouldn't improv in the play. It doesn't need to be heated but it should be jarring for an audience. They should be guessing if

*this is scripted or not. Eventually, they come to an agreement to 'Put a pin in it for now',
and then…*

HAL: Shall we start?

GEORGE: Which bit is the start again?

HAL: We were gonna let the audience decide.

GEORGE: Maybe that's not a good idea. You know what they can be like.

HAL: Won't the theatre be annoyed?

GEORGE: I'm sure they won't mind, we'll tell them in advance and it'll
be fine.

HAL: Let's get this show on the road!

    GEORGE *comes to the front of the stage.*

    HAL *grabs the rope in the meantime, they prepare.*

C. HELMETS AND BALLOONIES!   STYLE: LAUREL AND HARDY

GEORGE: *Part A. Hope. Scene 1*

SANS: SANS *enters the space.*

MOINS: MOINS *enters the space.*

SANS: *They are tethered together.*

    The characters tie themselves in via the tether.

MOINS: *They sit facing the audience.* **SANS** *is blowing up balloons.*

SANS: MOINS *is fixing together a pair of party hats.*

MOINS: *They're VERY excited!*

SANS: We're adequately excited.

MOINS: They're more excited than that, don't let them fool you.

SANS: It's moderately exciting.

MOINS: MOINS *reveals to the audience that it's a very big day today!*

SANS: SANS *disagrees and tells them it's no bigger than the last time this happened.*

    It's no bigger than the last time this happened.

MOINS: This time's different.

SANS: How so?

MOINS: We have helmets. We have balloonies.

SANS: Big day.

MOINS: We're getting saved today, you see.

SANS: Sure are.

MOINS: MOINS *is nearing the end of their tether:*

    Will you stop being such a Debbie downer!

SANS: Debbie who?

MOINS: Downer.

SANS: *I hardly know 'er!*

MOINS: Sans…

SANS: Moins.

MOINS: We have to hold onto something.

SANS: *(Referencing the tether.)* I know we bloody do.

MOINS: I mean more than that!

SANS: SANS *is fed up already.*

MOINS: Shall we start again?

SANS: We'd better had.

MOINS: And you promise you'll be more…

SANS: More?

MOINS: MOINS *pulls an overly ecstatic face.*

SANS: Yes, yes ok. Fine. I promise I'll try.

MOINS: Just promise.

SANS: I'll try.

MOINS: It'll have to do. Ok. Ready sailor?

SANS: Sailor?

MOINS: Trying it out.

SANS: Starboard, commander.

MOINS: What?!

SANS: Trying it out.

MOINS: *A look with appreciation in its heart.*

    MOINS *puts his thumb up.*

SANS: Come on then.

MOINS: Three. Two. One…

BREAK:

GEORGE: I think that was pretty good.

HAL: Mm yeah, not too bad.

GEORGE: Not too bad? Not too – Hal mate that was fucking sick. Did you see yourself? That was sick. They're going to love it.

They're going to absolutely love it.

HAL: Do you know when we finish today?

Beat.

GEORGE: What?

HAL: It's just…I've kinda got somewhere else to be.

GEORGE: Maybe we could try the fight bit super super quick?

I just feel like we haven't found the meaning yet.

HAL: What did you have in mind when you wrote the script?

GEORGE: It's not that easy.

HAL: Sure it is, just tell me the meaning and I'll do it.

GEORGE: Part A, scene three.

HAL: Are we doing that, then?

MOINS: MOINS *shoots daggers at* **SANS**.

HAL: I haven't got long.

MOINS: Do you wanna go?

HAL: Yes, I do.

GEORGE: No like, go. Like *go*. Like scrap?

HAL: Why would Sans want to scrap?

GEORGE: We're finding the meaning.

HAL: I haven't got the time.

GEORGE: Please?

HAL: Fine. But then I'm going.

GEORGE: And then you'll go.

> *The pair get back into position as* **SANS** *and* **MOINS**.
>
> **HAL** *forgets his line,* **GEORGE** *reminds him.*
>
> *Maybe they do a silly sequence of actions to get back in.*
>
> *BACK IN:*

SANS: Without me, you'd have nothing.

You can't hate the only thing you have.

MOINS: Maybe I do.

SANS: I can't hang my hopes on a maybe.

MOINS: Hopes of what?

SANS: You killing me. If you hate me.

MOINS: I wouldn't give you the satisfaction.

Stuck here. Endless. The void.

SANS: I'm sick of the void.

MOINS: We haven't spoken about that in ages!

SANS: Because there's nothing to chat about!

MOINS: Would you get hungry in the void?

SANS: I don't know, Moins. Because we aren't there.

MOINS: How do you know?

SANS: Because I've forgotten how we got here in the first place.

MOINS: I haven't.

SANS: Haven't you…

MOINS: Nope! I remember clear as day. Do you want to hear the story?

Sans? I know the story. I could tell the story if you –

SANS: Where's the message?

MOINS: The what?

SANS: The message.

MOINS: I dunno.

SANS: You don't know where the message is?

MOINS: No.

SANS: If we've lost the message, they won't accept us, surely!

MOINS: I'm not getting this, Sans.

Pause.

SANS: We need to give that message back when they collect us, how do you not understand that?

MOINS: Let's flip for it.

Another BREAK from the play.

Lights snap. **GEORGE** *turns the music off.*

HAL: No.

GEORGE: What now?

HAL: You've skipped! It's the wrong part of the story!

GEORGE: It's a cut I've made.

HAL: You can't just make cuts without telling me.

MOINS: MOINS *winks at the / audience*

HAL: No, no, NO. It's not fair. I liked that bit.

GEORGE: Oh, cry me a river.

HAL: That's when I got to do my serious acting.

GEORGE: You've got a juicy monologue later!

Beat.

HAL: What's my next line?

The pair head over to the script, they find the line.

HAL: Ok.

BACK IN:

SANS: I don't think this is a flipping situation, Moins.

What're we even flipping for?

MOINS: Peace of mind!

SANS: Brilliant. We all love peace of mind, don't we?

MOINS: Tails we needed the message to be saved, and we have every right to panic. Heads we didn't need it, and we can calm down, back to the celebrations.

SANS: Ok, ok. Alright. Tails for panic, Heads for worry less. Yes?

MOINS: Yes. Ready sailor?

SANS: At ease, soldier.

Pause.

SANS: Yes I'm ready!

MOINS: *Overly-dramatic music plays.*

    GEORGE *goes over to the tech desk.*

GEORGE: Shit.

HAL: What?

GEORGE: I haven't got the music in yet.

HAL: Oh.

GEORGE: I haven't downloaded it from YouTube yet.

HAL: Kinda important, though.

GEORGE: I know.

Beat.

GEORGE: Sorry.

A long and awkward pause. The pair aren't sure what to do.

HAL: I tell ya what, why don't I sing something for now so we can rehearse it and then we can think about –

GEORGE: Are you sure?

HAL: Yeah yeah and if it works we can put it in?

GEORGE: Yeah?

HAL: Yeah?

GEORGE: Would that be alright?

HAL: Yeah!

GEORGE: Alright, thanks mate, yeah. I'll give you the cue yeah? I'll, ok…

BACK IN:

MOINS: *Overly-dramatic music plays.*

    HAL *does a really shite beat.*

    Think Stomp but…shit.

MOINS: **MOINS** *flips the coin. It lands. Keeps it hidden from* **SANS***..*

SANS/HAL: What is it?

MOINS: WE'RE REALLY EXCITED!

SANS: WHAT DID IT LAND ON?

MOINS: WE'RE GETTING SAVED TODAY!

SANS: MOINS!

MOINS: AND THIS TIME IT'S REALLY DIFFERENT!

SANS: WHAT DID THE COIN SAY?

MOINS: IT'S REALLY HAPPENING!

    SANS *pulls on the tether, bringing* **MOINS** *to the floor.*

MOINS: HEADS! HEADS! IT WAS HEADS!

    SANS *lets* **MOINS** *go.*

SANS: You swear?

MOINS: Fuck.

SANS: No.

MOINS: What?

SANS: Swear.

MOINS: Shit.

SANS: No, that's not –

MOINS: You said swear.

SANS: You promise?

MOINS: Promises are dangerous things.

SANS: As are lies.

MOINS: I wouldn't lie to you.

SANS: I wouldn't lie to you either.

You promise it was heads?

MOINS: It's why I started again.

We can be excited again.

Suddenly, a timer goes off.

The pair are spooked.

BREAK OUT:

HAL: That must be my cue to leave then.

GEORGE: No it's not. Break time is what that is matey boy.

HAL: I need to go.

GEORGE: You can go on the next one, yeah? It'll only be for a little bit.

HAL: George, there'll be plenty more days like this one. And we don't want to do it to death now do we?

GEORGE: Yeah right. Practise makes perfect mate. We have to get this right.

HAL: And we will.

GEORGE: Today.

HAL: Till the next break.

GEORGE: Till the next break!

HAL: And then we'll get on with our lives.

GEORGE: We will, we will. I promise. But for now, relax. Break time, baby!

IMPROVISATION TWO:

The two actors should improv as mates. It should feel warm and honest. It could be about their previous experiences in the theatre industry. It could be about the best bits of the play. It could be about James Acaster. The main things to note should be that balloons should be blown up during the scene, and party hats should be put on. The pair should end the improv playing the game where the balloon must be kept in the air, where the conversation comes to...

GEORGE: Hal?

HAL: Yeah?

GEORGE: Do you think we're any good?

HAL: Yeah.

GEORGE: Do you think *they'll think* we're any good?

HAL: Do you think you're good?

GEORGE: I think so.

HAL: Then why're you worried?

GEORGE: Do you not worry?

HAL: Way I see it, you can be a worrier in life, or you can be a warrior in life.

Are you a worrier, or warrior, my friend?

GEORGE: Can I be a worry warrior?

HAL: You can be whatever you like, kid.

GEORGE: Thanks, Dad.

HAL: No, I wasn't...no that wasn't –

GEORGE: You're like a Dad to me.

HAL: Why're you –

GEORGE: Am I like your son?

Out to the audience, taking the piss out of the convention.

HAL: Is this hell? Am I in hell, stuck with you?

GEORGE: I think it's a bit worse than hell, where we are now, matey!

HAL: What do you mean?

Nothing.

HAL: George?

GEORGE: Do you not remember?

HAL: What're you on about?

GEORGE *ties themselves back in.*

HAL: Don't you dare. You can't just / avoid

D | OUR LOVELY, LOVELY WORK

GEORGE: Part A, Scene 5

HAL: No, tell me what you mean.

GEORGE: Let's do the play, and you'll figure it out, ok?

Part A, Scene 5

MOINS: *SANS and **MOINS** have made up after a brief interlude of trust issues.*

SANS: *They've got onto the topic of work!*

MOINS: *They're having a very nice time explaining what they do to the audience.*

SANS: Our line of work can be very…

MOINS: Curious, sometimes,

BOTH: You see…

SANS: sometimes we don't like to talk about it.

MOINS: As it's difficult to know what to say!

SANS: People always ask us questions.

MOINS: Well, not anymore they don't.

SANS: We don't see many, when we're here, you see.

MOINS: But it brings us to places like this! Which is

BOTH: Nice.

SANS: Yes, at times,

BOTH: You see

MOINS: we're in the business of serving!

HAL: Is that what you've written in?

GEORGE: Yeah.

HAL: We don't serve.

GEORGE: We do.

HAL: Who?

GEORGE: The audience.

HAL: Fuck the audience.

GEORGE: Hal! No swearies please.

HAL: Can we change that line?

GEORGE: Really?

HAL: Yeah. Let Sans say it.

GEORGE: Ok…

BACK IN:

SANS: We're in the business of storytelling.

MOINS: Bit wanky!

SANS: We're in the business of statement making.

MOINS: Bit tory!

SANS: WE'RE IN THE BUSINESS OF –

MOINS: – CONSTANT WORRY.

Beat.

HAL: Let's move on.

GEORGE: Can we do my favorite bit?

HAL: We always do that bit.

BACK IN:

GEORGE and **HAL** *take up positions staring out at the beach.*

Think over-egged GCSE Drama. Think big breaths, big sighs.

Think talking in a way that no one talks like.

Half-way between epic theatre and David Attenborough.

MOINS: Part A, scene seven.

SANS: *SANS* and **MOINS** *are staring out blankly.*

MOINS: *It's oddly peaceful, and yet ominous. Or at least, that's what the audience think about this particular scene.*

SANS: *SANS isn't sure how the playwright can dictate what the audience might think.*

MOINS: *MOINS thinks SANS should stay in their lane.*

SANS: *SANS thinks MOINS should start the scene how it's meant to.*

MOINS: *MOINS starts* **GEORGE'***s favourite bit.*

Four clicks or stamps.

The next few lines are said in a rhythm.

MOINS: You really don't remember how we got here?

SANS: Of course not.

MOINS: I don't understand.

SANS: You don't understand much.

MOINS: But I do understand how we got here.

The pair move positions in the "wind".

SANS: *The pair pause for reflection. After a pregnant pause…*

The rhythm returns.

SANS: We have to hold onto something.

MOINS: We do. You're right.

SANS: I'm always right.

MOINS: Sans?

SANS: Moins.

MOINS: I love you.

SANS: You don't know what that means.

MOINS: It's just something nice to say.

> *Beat.* **GEORGE** *goes in for a kiss…*

HAL: Ok, now can we do my favourite bit?

GEORGE: We didn't get to finish mine!

HAL: I think there is as good of a place to end as any.

GEORGE: Who's writing this thing?

HAL: Do you even know?

GEORGE: Let's get this over with then. Come on, up you get, actor boy.

BACK IN:

GEORGE: SANS *takes up an acting position. This is the most serious they've ever been. This is a serious monologue, for a serious actor in a serious play, in –*

HAL: Can you just let me do it?

MOINS: SANS *has awoken.* **MOINS** *is still snoring, cuddling the tether.*

   MOINS *snores.* **SANS** *stands.* **GEORGE** *starts the music.*

   HAL *takes up his position.*

SANS: I dreamt about it again. It was there.

   The…the void. Not that I'd tell Moins. But it's real. It's there.

   There are two ants, carrying a load on their back.

   The load speaking every now and then, instructing them.

   Spitting out random words, random orders, random things.

   Hundreds of them, only in spurts. Only at certain times.

   All in darkness. In an inky well, unavoidable.

   An inevitability.

   Two ants, carrying a load on their back.

   Round and round and round and round and round.

   Again and again and again.

   Circles.

   Because it's dark, you see, and they can't see where they're going.

   They don't know.

   All they can feel is each other, connected through this load they have.

   All they have is one another.

   Nothing else, in the darkness.

Emotion, thought, feeling.

Nothing more, nothing less.

Eventually, they're crushed. And I wake up.

But they live again, in the next dream.

And here I am, again.

GEORGE: Great! // Great!

How did that feel?

IMPROVISATION THREE:

GEORGE *gives* **HAL** *some notes on their monologue. It's obviously a sore spot. For context, they've worked on this section a lot.* **GEORGE** *wants to push the monologue further, heighten it, play it bigger.* **HAL** *wants to be Timothèe Chalamet in Call Me by Your Name.* **GEORGE** *could try to convince* **HAL** *that it should be a hybrid physical theatre moment. It should end in…*

HAL: I just think the imperfections are what make it, yano, like –

GEORGE: Yeah but we need to be perfect, don't we?

HAL: You're making this really difficult for me.

GEORGE: It's my working method, baby!

HAL: Your notes are counterproductive.

GEORGE: Yeah? Well maybe if you listened to me once in a while, we wouldn't be in this mess, would we?

HAL: Are we in a mess? What's the mess?

G | THE RETURN OF THE FLIPS   STYLE: GAMESHOW

GEORGE: Part B, Loss. Scene three.

> **GEORGE** *plays the music. It could be gameshow related.*
>
> *It could be FLASH GORDON.*

HAL: So that's what we're doing now then?

MOINS: Another flip! To see if they'll be saved. It must be done!

SANS: What doth we flip for squire?

MOINS: To move, or not to move!

HAL: I thought this bit was about getting saved.

GEORGE: It is. In the end. *(As* **MOINS.***):* TO MOVE, OR NOT TO
MOVE!

SANS: That is the question!

GEORGE: What?

SANS: *That,* is the question!

MOINS: Heads for stay put, tails for runaway from the creators –

HAL: Who're the creators?

GEORGE: The creatives, us.

HAL: Why're they running from us?

GEORGE: They might be cut –

MOINS: Tails we run-away from the creators and save ourselves.

SANS: Heads for stick, Tails for scatter!

MOINS: Who will flip our lucky flipper?

SANS: Our lucky flipper is very flippable!

MOINS: We need a flipper!

SANS: A flipper is what we need!

MOINS: Come on down!

SANS: Come on down!

MOINS: Come on…

SANS: Come on…

MOINS: Come…

I don't think they're gonna do it.

BRIEF IMPROVISATION:

The pair decide they shouldn't get an audience member up onstage. Comments about the audience member being funnier than them or looking at the actors and thinking 'fuck that' would suffice. It should end with the pair deciding to do it themselves instead.

MOINS: MOINS *flips the coin.*

SANS: *A moment of palpable tension.*

MOINS: *It spins twenty, maybe thirty times in the air.*

SANS: *It's like watching a ballerina on a helter-skelter.*

MOINS: *The coin lands back in* **MOINS**' *hands after an arduous journey.*

SANS: What did it land on?

MOINS: Heads! We stick!

SANS: We stick?

MOINS: We stick, but we prepare a map for when we go someday!

SANS: The coin said all that?

MOINS: When you know how to read it, you just know!

SANS: We will get out of here some day…

MOINS: The saviors will come for us!

SANS: As long as we stay put for now!

MOINS: The coiny coin said so!

SANS: We're getting out of here.

MOINS: Together, yes?

Beat.

GEORGE: Together, yes?

Beat.

MOINS: A restart. I believe.

HAL: Really?

MOINS: A restart.

HAL: I don't want to. I need to go.

MOINS: What you want and what we have to do are two very different things.

HAL: What are you talking about?

MOINS: You have no say in what you do.

Your every move calculated already. Destiny. By them, up there.

The Creators.

A thousand eyes watching. Waiting.

HAL: There definitely won't be a thousand out there.

GEORGE: One day there might be.

HAL: The playwright has big thoughts of themselves.

GEORGE: Can you just do the fucking script so we can get out of here please.

HAL: We can get out of here whenever.

GEORGE: That's what you think, yeah?

HAL: I can leave out of that door whenever I want.

GEORGE: So why haven't you yet?

> **HAL** *walks off in a huff.*

> **GEORGE** *is left trying to hold it together as* **MOINS**. *Maybe they coil the rope.*

MOINS: It has to mean something.

If we are here, in this place, at this point in time, and we mean nothing, we're just *here* then…we are nothing. We have nothing.

We go round, again. Without anything left.

And if that's the case, then all we truly have is one another.

And if that's the case, our hope can only be within ourselves.

Our routines.

We must stick, to scatter.

You see?

HAL: I'm not restarting.

MOINS: We have to get this right, *Sans.*

We're celebrating.

SANS: I HATE THIS BLOODY TETHER.

MOINS: I DON'T. IT MAKES ME FEEL CLOSER TO YOU.

BREAK.

The pair are caught in an awkward admission.

HAL: We can't just constantly restart.

GEORGE: Who says we can't? They don't get saved if we don't restart.

HAL: Moins loses the message. Could we try that?

GEORGE: No. The play is about hope. There's no hope without the message.

HAL: Hope is flimsy.

GEORGE: But the play is about hope.

HAL: I'm not restarting.

GEORGE: Then we continue.

HAL: I can't keep going on and on and on until the end of bloody time.

GEORGE: You still ain't getting it yet are you?

HAL: Getting what?

GEORGE: Part A. Hope. Scene 12.

The pair fall asleep to silly music, sleeping with over-the-top snores.

MOINS: MOINS *awakens with a yawn.*

SANS: SANS *awakens with a yawn.*

SANS: Where were we again?

MOINS: Somewhere in the middle.

SANS: We're getting there quick, aren't we.

MOINS: We're getting there pretty quick.

SANS: Oh, yes. Hi.

MOINS: Did you forget about them?

SANS: No, not at all. Hi.

MOINS: We've been getting along great, haven't we? Eurgh.

SANS: What?

MOINS: It's wet.

SANS: No it's not.

MOINS: It is.

SANS: You're lying.

MOINS: Did Sans have a little trickle?

SANS: SANS DID NOT.

MOINS: Sans *definitely* trickled.

HAL: SANS DID NOT TRICKLE.

MOINS: No need to shout. You'll slip in the trickle if you aren't cautious!

SANS: Where's the coiny coin?

MOINS: The coiny coin?

SANS: We can flip to find out who trickled.

MOINS: You had it.

HAL: You're kidding.

GEORGE: Can you play your part please.

SANS: You're kidding!

MOINS: It'll be around here somewhere. I promise you.

SANS: You're always losing things. You're always…

MOINS: I wish you'd leave me alone every once in a while.

SANS: I literally can't.

MOINS: You've never tried.

SANS : That's what you think.

    I'd leave you in a heartbeat.

    Trust me.

    Pause.

SANS: Where've you left it?

SANS: SANS *tries to search for coiny coin.*

MOINS: MOINS *won't budge.*

SANS: I need to search.

MOINS: Take that back. Now.

SANS: We need that coin, Moins.

MOINS: MWANS. MWANS. IT'S PRONOUNCED, MWAAAANS!

SANS: FINE! MWANS! MWANS! MWAAAANS!

    The pair are pulling on the tether, both creating a tension which leads to a great deal of physical exertion. **SANS** *trying to leave to find the coin,* **MOINS** *to stop.*

SANS: Stop stopping me!

MOINS: You wouldn't leave me!

SANS: I would!

MOINS: We're in this together.

SANS: LITERALLY, WE ARE.

GEORGE: CAN YOU JUST DO THE CORRECT LINES PLEASE.

HAL: I'M DOING THE FUCKING LINES.

GEORGE: JUST DO IT PROPERLY AND WE CAN LEAVE.

HAL: I DON'T WANNA DO THIS SHITE PLAY ANYMORE.

GEORGE: CAN YOU JUST FUCK OFF THEN.

The timer goes off again. Loud.

IMPROVISATION FOUR:

Could be like this bit of Star Wars The Phantom Menace where Darth Maul, Obi and Qui-Gon Jinn are staring each other down through the red screens in-between the fight.

A heated tension that's unspoken. Long, silent.

GEORGE *tries to put up a party banner at the back of the stage.*

GEORGE *can't put it up on their own.* **HAL** *should leave it for a while, before helping put it up with tape.*

GEORGE: …thanks.

They finish putting it up. A step towards a bridge being rebuilt.

GEORGE: You have to get it right, you know.

HAL: What're you on about now?

GEORGE: To get out of here, to get out of this place.

There've been ones like you before.

HAL: You're a perfectionist. You just want to get things right.

GEORGE: They don't let you out until we do. Do you really wanna go out there underprepared?

HAL: I know the story.

GEORGE: Do you really though?

Beat.

GEORGE: If you get it right, you leave. If you don't, we do it again.

And again. And again. Time after time, until you're allowed to go.

Until you're saved.

HAL: Moins?

GEORGE: George.

A long pause.

GEORGE: So. Ready?

Nothing.

GEORGE: Ready, Sailor?

HAL: Is there an end?

GEORGE: You just wait and see.

GEORGE: *TETHERED: A Play with Stage Directions.*

SANS: SANS *enters the space.*

MOINS: MOINS *enters the space.*

> *They are tethered together.*

> *The pair tether themselves together.*

SANS: SANS *stands, holding a map.*

SANS/ MOINS: This way!

> EURGH

> No!

> *The pair tut and shake their heads. They swap positions:*

SANS / MOINS: This way!

> EURGH

> No!

MOINS: How come you know the way all of a sudden?

SANS: Because I made this map in this first place.

> *(To audience.)* I made this map in the first place, you see.

> It's very intricate. It's very complex.

MOINS: They like to think it's more complicated than it is, you see.

SANS: You see, they don't get it.

MOINS: I do, it's not that complex. It's a map.

SANS: We've been working on this map for some time.

MOINS: They've been working on it more than me.

SANS: That's not true! We've worked on it together, you see.

MOINS: It was their idea.

SANS: We both wanted to do this.

MOINS: Do you think the map actually helps with anything?

SANS: Do you not want to be saved?

MOINS: I do. I do…

SANS: Why're you questioning it then?

MOINS: I'm not, I'm not.

SANS: This will help us find our way to the savior or help us escape. It's every person for themselves if it comes down to it.

MOINS: Oi.

SANS: I want to get out of here, whether they're with me or not.

MOINS: I'd never leave you.

SANS: I'd leave you.

MOINS: We might not need to leave.

This might be where we're supposed to be.

SANS: Don't go having doubts on me now.

MOINS: It might be better here than it is over there. In that greener place.

SANS: Greener?

MOINS: Old tongue.

SANS: *Greener.*

MOINS: You're all I've got. And I'm all you've got.

Pause.

SANS: This way.

MOINS: You've got it up the wrong way.

SANS: I don't.

MOINS: They do.

SANS: I made the thing!

MOINS: But look, the co-ordinates are –

SANS: Let's just –

MOINS: Look it's all wrong!

SANS: Let's just move in a –

MOINS: We're going the completely opposite –

SANS: Let's just move in a direction –

MOINS: Let's just move in a direction and I'm sure we'll find our way.

SANS: And if we don't?

MOINS: More time spent together.

    Pause.

SANS: Aye aye sailor.

MOINS: Sailor? What is that?

SANS: Sailor?

MOINS: No, why're you saying it?

SANS: Fun thing to say.

MOINS: "Aye aye…sailor."

SANS: We're losing light, come on.

MOINS: *The light changes. The pair begin their journey for salvation.*

SANS: *Over the top, heroic music plays.*

MOINS: What was that! On the floor back there!

    It looked like balloonies and helmets!

SANS: Come on. COME ON!

    The less time we take, the less time until we're saved.

MOINS: SANS *drags* **MOINS** *along.*

Silence for a –

SANS: Just let it happen.

Quiet. Long.

MOINS: Sans?

SANS: Moins.

MOINS: Do you think we'll ever be free?

SANS: We can only hope.

MOINS: Hope. Yes.

SANS: Hope is all we have.

MOINS: Flimsy.

SANS: Not now.

MOINS: I hope we get out of here together.

SANS: I hope we get out of here.

MOINS: I hope.

SANS: I hope.

MOINS: MOINS *notices it's getting darker. The pair have no idea where they are.*

SANS: I know where we are.

MOINS: Do you?

SANS: I know exactly…where…we…um.

MOINS: We should've stayed put.

SANS: We can't just sit around hoping to be saved. We had the message.

MOINS: We don't anymore.

SANS: We have a map.

MOINS: And where's that got us.

SANS: We have the coin flips! They told us what to do!

MOINS: The coin flip told us to stick.

SANS: We can't just lose hope like this.

MOINS: We lost that a long time ago.

SANS: They're over exaggerating.

MOINS: They're being optimistic.

SANS: They need to stop.

MOINS: I have.

> *Over the following, kid* **MOINS** *blurs back into* **GEORGE**.

MOINS: Is it better to go round in circles,

Safe, safe in the knowledge of consistency,

Than it is to breach into the unknown,

Unaware of anything that lies in store for you?

I don't think there's a saviour out there for us.

I don't think anyone can be saved, not really.

I don't think there's any hope out there for anyone.

Anyone at all. Which is why we have to keep hold of each other.

Your dream, there's always two ants. Two. Not one, two.

Dependent on each other for survival.

Maybe that's the real savior we've been searching for.

SANS: No.

MOINS: No?

SANS: We need to be saved to have something to hold onto.

To have anything at all.

MOINS: In my version of the dream, one ant is crushed.

Crushed under a darkened boot, while the other runs free.

How could the other live properly, knowing what it's left behind?

SANS: YES!

YEEEES!

MOINS: What? What do you mean, yes?

SANS: There's an end!

MOINS: In the dream, yes.

SANS: Dreams are just reality sleeping.

MOINS: We're not ants.

SANS: It's all the same.

MOINS: I'm not an ant. Are you an ant?

SANS: Do I look like an ant?

MOINS: You probably will to them.

A little bug. Playing around in front of them.

Forgotten about in an hour's time. That's all we are.

SANS: Let's hope so.

MOINS: Characters in a story. And where do we go after?

Pause.

MOINS: What's out there after all this?

SANS: Flip.

MOINS: For?

SANS: Getting saved.

MOINS: Flip for the saviours?

SANS: The almighty saviours.

Heads for saved.

MOINS: Tails for none.

SANS: MOINS *flips.*

MOINS: *It lands.*

SANS: *They both look at it.*

GEORGE *hides it from* **HAL.**

MOINS: I don't think they're coming.

I don't think they're coming at all.

SANS: Not all hope is lost.

MOINS: It was Tails.

The coin, it was tails. I'm sorry.

SANS: SANS *is confused.*

MOINS: MOINS *is sorry.*

SANS: They aren't coming.

MOINS: They aren't.

I've lied to you.

You trusted me, and I lied.

SANS: I never trusted you. I don't know what it means.

MOINS: All the times before, it was the opposite

We were supposed to move.

We needed the message.

Tails. Every flip.

Pause. Long.

SANS: Not heads?

MOINS: Headless. Like a Rooster.

SANS: Chicken.

MOINS: What?

SANS: Headless chicken.

> **MOINS** *dismisses with a hand.*

L | THIS IS OUR FINAL MOMENT   STYLE: MOINS AND HAL

SANS: Fuck this.

MOINS: No swearies please!

SANS: I do remember how we got here.

A long and hard journey.

Through many rooms, many faces, telling us we were wrong, telling us we were right.

The Creators.

They put us here, and we went with them.

And now they have us in this… circle. Nowhere to go apart from around

And around again.

And that's why we need to leave.

We need to give up.

MOINS: I'm not following.

SANS: Sometimes we need to forget where we've come from

To keep going forward. Do you see?

MOINS: I see.

SANS: You see.

MOINS: I don't see.

HAL: No more restarts.

MOINS: No.

HAL: No more do-overs.

MOINS: No.

HAL: We just…carry on. Alone.

MOINS: NO!

We've worked too hard to just leave it all now.

HAL: Find comfort in knowing we tried our hardest.

MOINS: We've come too far. I'm not having this shit we, we

We need a message! We need to know why, we need-

HAL: Give it a rest, George.

MOINS: MOINS MOINS! I'M MOINS, OK?

HAL: We need to get on with our lives –

MOINS: Back, we go back, we get it right, we get it right

Together

This is all about us

Together.

HAL: Let's just sit down and rationally / talk about what…

MOINS: NO. You want to destroy something beautiful.

HAL: You're being ridiculous.

MOINS: Would you kill your own child?

HAL: Look, I thought about what you said –

MOINS: AND I THOUGHT ABOUT WHAT YOU SAID!

WE ARE GETTING SAVED!

WE ARE GETTING SAVED! FROM THIS PLACE! FROM HERE!

WE ARE! TOGETHER!

MOINS *BEGINS RUNNING, DRAGGING* **SANS** *ALONG BEHIND VIA THE TETHER!*

MOINS *does so. It should be animalistic, desperate, the last attempt at hope.*

HAL: George.

MOINS: I KNOW WHAT YOU'RE TRYING TO DO.

HAL: Stop.

MOINS: AND IT WON'T WORK!

HAL: Please.

GEORGE: YOU WON'T DO WHAT EVERYONE ELSE DOES!

SANS: SANS *unties themselves.*

HAL: More to life.

Long pause.

GEORGE: There's nothing else for me.

HAL: There's plenty else.

GEORGE: *We're* all I have. This is all I have.

SANS: We need a decision. A decision is what we need.

    MOINS *retrieves the coin.*

SANS: Mwans retrieves the coin.

MOINS: Heads, tether.

SANS: Tails, together, but apart.

    GEORGE/MOINS *flips the coin. It lands. They don't look at it.*

SANS: To be saved.

Long pause.

MOINS: A restart.

The timer goes off. Loud.

MOINS: Please?

I need us to stay, because I don't know what else is out there, ok?

I can't do it on my own, I can't…

Sans? Hal?

Long pause. The timer is going crazy.

GEORGE: One more go. Yeah? One more go.

Blackout.

The lights come back up, the dance sequence from the beginning.

It is unclear if the play has restarted, and the characters are going around again, or if this is the curtain call, and the play has finished.

And that's how the hour with the audience finishes.

END.

Tethered Reviews

OFFcom Short Run Award | WINNER

London Pub Theatres | Standing Ovation| NOMINATED

★★★★★ "A laugh-out-loud surreal comedy… with layers of nuance and thought-provoking moments which leave the audience questioning who they are." | **London Theatre 1**

★★★★★ "ChewBoy Productions are once again on top form – funny, clever, inventive and original." | **The Review Chap**

★★★★ "The sort of theatre you can fall in love with." | **View from the Outside**

★★★★ "An engrossing play which successfully builds on a history of performance to create something new and exciting." | **London Pub Theaters**

★★★★ "An extremely clever example of new work that Fringe theatres can be proud to host." | **Elaine Chapman**

Chewboy Productions Reviews

**Best of Brighton Fringe Award 2019
(EUAN) | WINNER**

★★★★★

"ChewBoy Productions are a theatrical force to be reckoned with." | **The Review Chap (EUAN 2018)**

★★★★

"The one-hour running time flew by and there were many genuine laugh-out-loud moments." | **LondonTheatre1 (EUAN, 2018)**

★★★★

"Brave, baffling and brilliant to boot."
| **Broadway Baby (EUAN, 2018)**

★★★★

"EUAN could soon be following Fleabag's footsteps as a fringe show turned masterpiece."
Voice Magazine (EUAN, 2019)

★★★★

"Wonderfully avant-garde, open to countless different interpretations." | **Everything Theatre (THE PROCESS TRILOGY, 2019)**

★★★★

"An ambitious, unique company unafraid to embrace the delightfully weird." | **Movie Burner (THE ZIZZ, 2021)**

★★★★

"a breathless surrealist caper that is sustained by its own unimpeachable internal logic" | **Spy in the Stalls (EUAN, 2019)**

"Downright bewildering, but also bloody brilliant."
| **Views from the Gods (EUAN, 2019)**

"Even when dealing with incredibly weighty issues, ChewBoy's approach is one that is adept in its addition of comical charm and whimsy" | **Miro Magazine (THE PROCESS TRILOGY, 2019)**

★★★★

"dark, ridiculous and brazenly charming, EUAN is a truly peerless invention"
BN1 Magazine (EUAN, 2019)